JOYFULLY SHARING THE GOSPEL

JOYFULLY SHARING
THE GOSPEL:

AN INTRODUCTION TO
EVANGELII GAUDIUM

DESMOND O'DONNELL O.M.I.

the columba press

First published in 2014 by
the columba press
55a Spruce Avenue,
Stillorgan Industrial Park,
Blackrock, Co. Dublin

ISBN 978–1–78218–180–4

Cover design by David Mc Namara C.Ss.R.
Origination by The Columba Press
Printed by ScandBook AB

Contents

Preface

With this small book I would like to both introduce you to Pope Francis' new message, *Evangelii Gaudium* (*The Joy of the Gospel*) and to enhance your understanding of his exhortation to all Catholics and Christian people.

This appeal by Pope Francis is an exhilarating one. It is a passionate call to relish God's love and to enjoy spreading it to others. His message is groundbreaking.

I will introduce you to the Pope's words, and guide you through its central message in two ways.

Firstly, I have selected central quotations from almost every paragraph, and within each, I have created an emphasis, to give it more immediacy. This is shown in bold, creating an instant link between key words and the full text. The number references at the end of each paragraph are for ease of referral to the original text.

Secondly, I have also created a comprehensive index to the themes and subjects of Pope Francis' complete text.

My hope is that, above all, this book will be both your guide to reading *Evangelii Gaudium* and a useful tool to enrich your study of the Pope's great exhortation.

Chapter One

Joy in Sharing the Gospel

Right at the beginning, Pope Francis' message is clear – when we have good news, we have a strong urge to tell others and to hope that they can share in it. The greatest good news for all of us is to know that we are loved by one or many. Since a Christian is someone who has the experiences of being loved by Jesus, he or she always wishes to help others towards the same experience. Being loved by Jesus means that we are sure of constant forgiveness and strengthened to endure even great suffering. Inviting others to have this experience is sharing the joy of the Gospel.

The joy of the Gospel fills the hearts and lives of all who **encounter Jesus**. [1]

The great danger in today's world, pervaded as it is by consumerism, is the desolation and **anguish born of a complacent yet covetous heart**. [2]

Whenever **our interior life** becomes caught up in its own interests and concerns, there is no longer room for others, no place for the poor. [2]

I invite all Christians, everywhere, at this very moment, to a renewed personal **encounter with Jesus Christ**. [3]

Let me say this once more: **God never tires of forgiving us**; we are the ones who tire of seeking his mercy ... Time and time again he bears us on his shoulders. [3]

No one can strip us of the dignity bestowed upon us by **God's boundless unfailing love**. [3]

I find it thrilling to reread this text: 'The Lord, your God is in your midst, a warrior who gives you the victory; he will rejoice over you with gladness, he will renew you in his love; **he will exult over you** with loud singing, as on the day of festival.' *Zephaniah 3:17* [4]

'My child, **treat yourself well**, according to your mean ... Do not deprive yourself of the day's enjoyment.' *Sirac 14:11* What **tender paternal love** echoes in these words! [4]

The Gospel, radiant with the glory of Christ's cross, constantly **invites us to rejoice** ... Why should we not also enter into this great stream of joy? [5]

I understand the grief of people who have **to endure great suffering,** yet slowly but surely we all have to let the joy of faith slowly revive, as a quiet yet firm trust, even amid the greatest distress. [6]

Joy adapts and changes, but always endures, even as a flicker of light born of our personal certainty that, when everything is said and done, **we are infinitely loved.** [6]

Technological society has succeeded in multiplying occasions of pleasure, yet has found it very difficult to engender joy. [7]

'Being a Christian is not the result of an ethical choice or a lofty idea, but the **encounter with an event, a person,** which gives life a new horizon and a decisive direction'. *Pope Benedict* [7]

Thanks solely to the encounter – or renewed **encounter – with God's love,** which blossoms into an enriching friendship, we are liberated from our narrowness and self-absorption. [8]

We become **fully human** when we become more than human, when we let God bring us beyond ourselves in order to attain the fullest truth of our being. [8]

Any person who has experienced **a profound liberation** becomes more sensitive to the needs of others. [9]

Life grows by being given away, and it weakens in isolation and comfort. Indeed, those who enjoy life most are those who leave security on the shore and become excited by the mission of communicating life to others. *Latin American Bishops* [10]

When the Church summons Christians to take up the task of **evangelisation,** she is simply pointing to the source of **authentic personal fulfilment.** [10]

Eternal Newness
A renewal of preaching can offer believers, as well as the lukewarm and the non-practicing, new joy in the faith. [11]

With this freshness he [Christ] is always able to renew our lives and our communities, and even if the Christian message has known periods of **darkness and ecclesial weakness,** it will never grow old. [11]

The life of the Church should always reveal clearly that **God takes the initiative,** that 'he has loved us first' *1 John 4:19* and that he alone 'gives the growth'. *1 Corinthians 3:7* [12]

God **asks everything** of us, yet at the same time he **offers everything** to us. [12]

Jesus leaves us **the Eucharist** as the Church's daily remembrance of, and deeper sharing in, the event of the Passover. *Luke 22:19* [13]

The believer is essentially 'one who remembers'. [13]

New evangelisation is animated by the fire of the Spirit, so as to inflame the hearts of the **faithful who regularly take part in community worship.** [15]

In the new evangelisation, we can also include those members of the faithful who preserve a deep and sincere faith, expressing it in different ways, but **seldom taking part in worship.** [15]

Instead of seeming to **impose new obligations**, Christians should appear as people who wish to share their joy, who point to a horizon of beauty and who invite others to a delicious banquet. [7]+[15]+[39]

Many of those who do not know Jesus Christ or who always rejected him are quietly seeking God … even in countries of ancient Christian tradition. [15]

It is not by proselytising that the Church grows, but **by attraction.** [15]

We cannot passively **wait in our church buildings;** we need to move from a pastoral ministry of mere conservation to a decidedly missionary pastoral ministry. [15]

The scope and limits of this Exhortation
Nor do I believe that **the papal magisterium** should be expected to offer a definitive or complete word on every question which affects the Church and the world. [16]

It is not advisable for the Pope to take the place of **local Bishops** in the discernment of every issue which arises in their territory. In this sense, I am conscious of the need to promote a sound **decentralisation.** [16]

Chapter Two

The Church is Missionary

Throughout his letter, the Pope tells us that the first step in helping others to God is to become lovingly involved in their lives. The parish is an ideal community in which everyone can do this by sharing with and encouraging others. The Pope and the bishops can encourage this loving by listening to everyone. People must not be put off by too many precepts, or by Church leaders becoming harsh judges or by the imposition of too many obligations. Pope Francis says that he likes it when the Church becomes 'bruised, hurting, dirty' 'through this loving involvement'.

God's word is unpredictable in its power ... The Church has to **accept this unruly freedom of the word** that accomplishes what it wills in ways that surpass our calculations and ways of thinking. [22]

Let us try a little harder **to become involved**. Jesus washed the feet of his disciples ... He tells his disciples: 'You will be blessed if you do this.' *John 13:17* [24]

7

The first step, being involved and supportive, bearing fruit and rejoicing

An evangelising community **gets involved by word and deed in people's daily lives**; it bridges distances, it is willing to abase itself if necessary, and it embraces human life, touching the suffering flesh of Christ in others. [24]

The Church evangelises and is herself evangelised through **the beauty of the liturgy**. [24]

I am aware that nowadays **documents** do not arouse the same interest as in the past, and that they are quickly forgotten. [25]

I hope that **all communities** will devote the necessary effort to advancing along the path of a **pastoral and missionary conversion** which cannot leave things as they presently are. Mere administration can no longer be enough. [25]

There are **ecclesial structures** which can hamper efforts at evangelisation, yet even good structures are only helpful when there is a life constantly driving, sustaining and assessing them. [26]

An ecclesial renewal which cannot be deferred
I dream of a missionary option that is an impulse
capable of transforming everything, so that the
**Church's customs, ways of doing things, times and
schedules, language and structures** can suitably be
channelled for the evangelisation of today's world
rather than for her self-preservation. [27]

The parish is not an outdated institution; precisely
because it possesses great flexibility, it can assume
quite different contours depending on the
openness and the missionary creativity of the
pastor the and community. [28]

If **the parish** proves capable of self-renewal and
constant adaptivity, it continues to be the Church
living in the midst of the homes of her sons and
daughters. This presumes that it really is in contact
with the homes and lives of its people, and does
not become a useless structure out of touch with
people or a self-absorbed group made up of a
chosen few. [28]

Other Church institutions, basic and small
communities, movements and forms of association
are a source of enrichment for the Church. [29]

The bishop … will have to encourage and develop the means of participation proposed in the Code of Canon Law, and … out of a desire to listen to everyone, and not simply to those who would tell him what he would like to hear. [31]

The principle aim of participatory processes should not be ecclesiastical organisation but rather the missionary aspiration of reaching everyone. [31]

Since I am called to put into practice what I ask of others, I too must think about a conversion of the papacy. It is my duty, **as the Bishop of Rome, to be open to suggestions** which can help make the exercise of my ministry more faithful to the meaning which Jesus Christ wished to give it … We have made little progress in this regard. [32]

Episcopal conferences are in a position to contribute in many and fruitful ways to the concrete realisation of the collegial spirit. Yet this desire has not been fully realised. Excessive centralisation … complicates the Church's life and her missionary outreach. [32]

Pastoral ministry in a missionary key seeks to abandon the complacent attitude that says: '**We have always done it this way.**' [33]

Instant communication and an occasionally biased media can lead to part of the church's **moral teaching being taken out of the context** which gives them meaning. The biggest problem is when the message we preach then seems identified with those secondary aspects. [34]

Pastoral ministry in a missionary style is not obsessed with the **disjointed transmission** of a multitude of doctrines to be insistently imposed … the message has to concentrate on the essentials. [35]

In Catholic doctrine there is an order or **a 'hierarchy' of truths** … This holds true for the dogmas of faith as for the whole corpus of the Church's teaching, including her moral teaching. [36]

What counts is 'faith working through love' (*Galatians 5:6*). 'The foundation of **the New Law is in the grace of the Holy Spirit,** who is manifested in the faith which works through love.' *St Thomas Aquinas* [37]

'In itself **mercy is the greatest of the virtues,** since all the others revolve around it and, more than this, it makes up for their deficiencies.' *St Thomas Aquinas* [38]

An imbalance occurs when … those virtues which ought to be most present in preaching and catechesis are overlooked. The same thing happens when we speak more about law than about grace, more about the Church than about Christ, more about the Pope than about God's word. [38]

When preaching is faithful to the Gospel, **the centrality of certain truths** is evident and it becomes clear that Christian morality is not a form of stoicism or self-denial. [39]+[7]

It is the task **of exegetes and theologians** to help the judgement of the Church to mature. [40]

Differing currents of thought in philosophy, theology and pastoral practice, if open to being reconciled by the Spirit in respect and love, can enable the Church to grow. [40]

[Some people] long for **a monolithic body of doctrine** guarded by all and leaving no room for nuance … but in fact, a variety serves to bring out and develop different facets of the inexhaustible riches of the Gospel. [40]

There are times when the faithful, in listening to completely orthodox language, take away something alien to the authentic Gospel of Jesus

Christ, because that **language is alien** to their own way of speaking to and understanding one another. [41]

We constantly seek ways of expressing unchanging truths in **a language** which brings out their abiding newness. [41]

Faith always remains something of **a cross**; it retains a certain obscurity which does not detract from the firmness of it assent. [42]

We need to remember that all religious teaching ultimately has to be reflected in **the teacher's way of life**. [42]

Certain customs not directly connected to the heart of the Gospel, even some with deep historical roots, are no longer properly understood and appreciated … We should not be afraid to re-examine them. [43]

St Thomas Aquinas pointed out that the precepts which Christ and the apostles gave to the people of God 'are very few'. [43]

The precepts enjoined by the Church, should be insisted on with **moderation**. [43]

The task of evangelisation operates within the
limits of language and of circumstances … without
renouncing the truth, the goodness and the light
which it can bring **whenever perfection is not
possible.** [45]

A missionary heart **never closes itself off,** never
retreats into its own security, never opts for **rigidity
and defensivness.** [45]

Often it is better to **slow down,** to put aside our
eagerness in order to see and listen to others. [46]

Pastors and the lay faithful who accompany their
brothers and sisters in faith or on the journey of
openness to God must always remember that
'**imputability and responsibility** for an action can
be diminished or even nullified by ignorance,
inadvertence, duress, fear, habit, inordinate
attachments or other psychological or social
factors'. *The Catholic Catechism 1735* [47]

The Church must go first not so much to our
friends and wealthy neighbours, but **above all to
the poor, and the sick,** those who are usually
despised and overlooked, 'those who cannot repay
you'. *Luke 14:14* [48]

I prefer a **Church that is bruised, hurting and dirty** because it has been out on the streets, rather than a Church that is unhealthy from being confined and from clinging to its own security. [49]

I do not want a Church concerned with being at the centre and then ends up being caught up in a web of **obsessions and procedures**. [49]

More than by fear of going astray, my hope is that we will be moved by the **fear of remaining shut up within structures** which give us a false sense of security, within rules which make us **harsh judges**, within habits which make us **feel safe**, while at our door people are starving and Jesus does not tire of saying to us: 'Give them something to eat.' *Mark 6:37* [49]

Chapter Three

External Challenges to Sharing the Gospel

Many people are anxious and afraid today because we are in a time of great and rapid change. Inhuman movements in economics have pushed many people to the fringe of society and made them mere things. The struggle for money, power and material things has led some to forgetfulness of God and to neglect of the human person. Corrupt financial systems have emerged. This is especially true in cities where loneliness and violence are on the increase. A Gospel-based education system that encourages critical thinking is necessary if marriage and family are to survive.

In our time humanity is experiencing **a turning point in its history** as we can see from the advances being made in many fields ... The hearts of many people are gripped by fear and desperation, even in so-called rich countries. [52]

No to an economy of exclusion
Masses of people find themselves **excluded and marginalised** without work, without possibilities, without any means of escape. [53]

Human beings are themselves considered consumer goods to be used and then discarded. We have created a disposable culture that is now spreading. [53]

Trickle down theories express a crude and naïve trust in the goodness of those wielding economic power. [54]

No to the new idolatry of money
A profound human crisis in a denial of the **primacy of the human person**. Man reduced to his needs alone; consumption. [55]

Today everything comes under the **laws of competition and survival of the fittest,** where the powerful feed upon the powerless. [55]

A profound human crisis: the denial of the primacy of the human person! ... man is reduced to one of his needs alone: consumption. [55]

The thirst for power and possessions knows no limit ... In this system whatever is fragile, like the environment, is defenceless before the interests of the deified market. [56]

No to a financial system that rules rather than serves
Corruption and self-serving tax evasion have taken on worldwide dimensions. [56]

Before this attitude – the autonomy of the marketplace – lurks **a rejection of ethics and a rejection of God.** [57]

The Pope loves everyone, rich and poor alike, but he is obliged in the name of Christ to remind all that **the rich must help, respect and promote the poor.** [58]

No to the inequality which spawns violence
When a society is willing to leave **a part of itself on the fringes,** no political programmes or resources spent on law enforcement or surveillance systems can indefinitely guarantee tranquillity. [59]

Some claim that the solution (to poverty) is **an 'education' that would tranquilise** them and make them tame and harmless. [60]

Some cultural challenges
In a culture where each person wants to be bearer of his or her own **subjective truth,** it becomes difficult for citizens to devise a common plan that transcends individual gain and personal ambitions. [61]

In the prevailing culture, priority is given to the outward, **the immediate, the visible, the quick, the superficial and the provisional.** What is real gives way to appearances. [62]

The Catholic faith of many peoples is nowadays being challenged by the proliferation of new religious movements, some of which tend to fundamentalism while others seem to propose **spirituality without God.** [63]

We are living in an **information-driven society** that bombards us indiscriminately with data – all treated as being of equal importance … that leads to remarkable superficiality in the area of moral development. [64]

Today we need to provide **an education that teaches critical thinking** and encourages the development of mature moral values. [64]

Despite the tide of secularism … **the Catholic Church is considered a credible institution** by public opinion, and trusted for solidarity and concern for those in greatest need. [65]

How much good has been done by Catholic **schools and universities** around the world! [65]

The family, the fundamental cell of society, is experiencing a profound cultural crisis, as are all communities and social bonds. [66]

Marriage tends to be viewed as a form of mere emotional satisfaction that can be constructed in any way or modified at will. [66]

The **individualism** of our post-modern and globalised era favours a lifestyle that weakens the development and stability of personal relationships and distorts family bonds. [67]

Challenges to inculturating the faith
We find among the most needy, a moral resource which preserves the values of an authentic Christian humanism. [68]

The immense importance of **a culture marked by faith cannot be overlooked**. [68]

Each culture and social group needs **purification and growth**. In the case of the popular cultures of Catholic peoples, we can see deficiencies that need to be healed by the Gospel. [69]

It is also true that at times greater emphasis is placed on the **outward expressions** and traditions of some group, or on alleged **private revelations** that could replace all else. [70]

Challenges from urban cultures
We need to **look at our cities with a contemplative gaze**, a gaze of faith that sees God dwelling in their homes, in their streets and squares. [71]

People in cities must often **struggle for survival** and this struggle contains within it a profound understanding of life that often includes a deep religious sense. [72]

A completely new culture has come to life, and continues to grow in our cities … Through the influence of the media, rural areas are being affected by the same cultural changes. [73]

Cities are the scene of **mass protests** where thousands of people call for freedom, a voice in public life, justice … which if not properly understood, will not be silenced by force. [74]

What could be significant places of encounter and solidarity often become **places of isolation and mutual mistrust.** [75]

We have to realise that **a uniform and rigid programme** of evangelisation is not suited to this (modern) complex reality. [75]

Chapter Four

Internal Challenges to Sharing the Gospel

The Pope recognises that the Church is making a great contribution to human welfare in these demanding times. However, even Christians can become selfish, lazy, small-minded and pessimistic. Jesus calls us to 'a revolution of tenderness' in communities of caring. All lay people have an irreplaceable contribution to make, and women whose rights and gifts are not recognised have much to offer in greater decision-making powers within the Church. Young people are admirable in their volunteer work for others. Together with elderly people, they must be listened to more.

The contribution of the Church in today's world is enormous … This witness comforts and sustains me in my own efforts to overcome selfishness and to give more fully of myself. [76]

I am aware that we need to **create spaces** where
pastoral workers can be helped and healed, places
where faith itself in the crucified Jesus is renewed;
where the most profound questions and daily
concerns are shared. [77]

Today we are seeing in many workers, including
consecrated men and women, an inordinate
concern for their personal freedom and relaxation,
which leads them to see their work as a mere
appendage to their life. [78]

One can observe in many agents of evangelisation,
even though they pray, a heightened **individualism,**
a crisis of identity and a cooling of fervour. [78]

At times our **media culture** and some intellectual
circles convey a marked scepticism with regard to
the Church's message. [79]

Pastoral workers can fall into a **relativism** … which
consists in acting as if God did not exist, making
decisions as if the poor did not exist, setting goals
as if others did not exist. [80]

No to selfishness and spiritual sloth
Many lay people fear that they may be asked to
undertake some apostolic work and they seek to

avoid any responsibility that may take them away from their free time … Something similar is also happening with **priests who are obsessed with protecting their free time**. [81]

[Apostolic work] can result in a state of **paralysis and acedia** because of activity undertaken badly, without adequate motivation, without a spirituality that would permeate it and make it pleasurable. [81] [82]

The biggest threat of all gradually takes shape: the **grey pragmatism** of the daily life of the church, in which all appears to proceed normally, while in reality faith is wearing down and degenerating into small-mindedness. [83]

[Among pastoral workers], **a tomb psychology** thus develops, and slowly transforms Christians into mummies in a museum. [83]

No to sterile pessimism
'Some see nothing but **prevarication** and ruin. We feel we must disagree with those prophets of doom who are always forecasting disaster … Divine Providence is leading us to a new order of human relations.' *John XXIII* [84]

The evil spirit of **defeatism** is brother to the temptation to separate, before its time, the wheat from the weeds; it is the fruit of an anxious and self-centred trust. [87]

In some places a spiritual '**desertification**' has evidently come about, as a result of attempts by some societies to build without God or to eliminate their Christian roots. [86]

Yes to a new relationship with Christ
To go out of ourselves and **to join others** is healthy for us. To be self-enclosed is to taste the bitter poison of immanence, and humanity will be worse for every selfish choice we make. [87]

The Christian ideal will always be a summons to overcome suspicion, habitual mistrust, **fear of losing our privacy**, all the defensive attitudes which today's world imposes on us. [88]

Some people want a **purely spiritual Christ**, without flesh and without a cross. [88]

They also want their interpersonal **relationships provided by sophisticated equipment**, by screens and systems which can be turned on and off on command. The Gospel tells us constantly to run the risk of a face-to-face encounter with others. [88]

The Son of God, by becoming flesh, summoned us to a **revolution of tenderness**. [88]

Isolation ... in the realm of religion can take the form of **spiritual consumerism** tailored to one's own unhealthy individualism. [89]

Genuine forms of **popular religiosity** are incarnate ... Their devotions are fleshy, they have a face. They are capable of fostering relationships and not just enabling escapism. [90]

In other parts of our society, we see the growing attraction to various forms of **spirituality of 'well-being'** divorced from any community life or to a 'theology of prosperity' detached from responsibility for our brothers and sisters. [90]

The solution will never be found in fleeing from a personal and committed **relationship with God** which at the same time commits us to serving others. [91]

Learning to find Jesus in the face of others, in their voices, in their pleas ... never tiring of our decision **to live in fraternity**. [91]

We are called to be witness to a constantly new way of living together in fidelity to the Gospel. Let us not allow ourselves to be robbed of **community**! [92]

No to spiritual worldliness
Spiritual worldliness, which hides behind the appearance of piety and even love of the Church, consists in seeking not the Lord's glory but human glory and personal well-being. [93]

Spiritual worldliness can be fuelled by … **a purely subjective faith** whose only interest is a certain experience of a set of ideas … imprisoned in one's own thoughts and feelings. [94]

Spiritual worldliness [can be expressed by] … those who ultimately trust in their own powers and feel superior to others because they observe certain rules or remain intransigently **faithful to a particular Catholic style from the past**. [94]

Spiritual worldliness can be seen in some people in whom we see an ostentatious **preoccupation for the liturgy, for doctrine and for the Church's prestige**. [95]

Spiritual worldliness can express itself in a
fascination with social and political gain, or pride
in their **ability to manage practical affairs** ...
Meetings, dinners, receptions, management,
statistics, plans and evaluation whose principal
beneficiary is not God's people but the Church as
an institution. [95]

We waste time **talking about what needs to done**
like spiritual masters and pastoral experts who give
instruction from on high ... We lose contact with
the real lives and the difficulties of our people. [96]

God save us from a worldly Church with
superficial spiritual and pastoral trappings ...
cloaks in outward religiosity bereft of God. Let us
not be robbed of the Gospel. [97]

No to warring among ourselves
Spiritual worldliness leads some Christians to war
with other Christians who stand in the way of
their **quest for power, prestige, pleasure and
economic security** ... a spirit of exclusivity. [98]

I ask Christians in communities throughout the
world, to offer a radiant and attractive **witness of
fraternal communion.** [99]

Beware of the temptation to **jealousy**! We are all in the same boat and headed for the same port! Let us ask for the grace to rejoice in the gifts of each other, which belong to all. [99]

It always pains me to discover how some Christian **communities**, and even consecrated persons, can tolerate different forms of enmity, division, calumny, defamation, vendetta, jealousy and the desire to impose certain ideas at all costs, even to persecutions which appear as veritable **witch hunts**. [100]

How much good it does to **love one another**, in spite of everything. [101]

To pray for **a person with whom I am irritated** is a beautiful step forward in love, an act of evangelisation … Let us not be robbed of the ideal of fraternal love. [101]

Other ecclesial challenges
Lay people are, put simply, the vast majority of the People of God. The minority – ordained ministers – are at their service. [102]

Room has not been made for **lay people to speak and to act**, due to excessive clericalism which keeps them away from decision-making. [102]

The Church acknowledges the indispensable contribution which **women** make to society ... We need to create still broader opportunities for a more incisive female presence in the Church. [103]

The **presence of women** must also be guaranteed in the workplace and in the various other settings where important decisions are made both in the Church and in social structures. [103]

Demands that the legitimate **rights of women** be respected ... present the Church with profound and challenging questions which cannot be lightly evaded. [104]

The reservation of priesthood to males ... Can prove especially divisive if sacramental power is too closely identified with power in general. [104]

As adults we find it difficult to listen patiently to them [**youth**], to appreciate their concerns and demands and speak to them in a language they can understand. [105]

Our efforts in the **field of education** do not produce the results expected. [105]

Despite the present crisis of commitment and communal relationships, many **young people** are making common cause before the problems of our world and are taking up various forms of activism and volunteer work. [106]

A dearth of vocations to priesthood and to the consecrated life is often due to a lack of contagious apostolic fervour in communities that results in a cooling of enthusiasm and attractiveness. [107]

Whenever we attempt to read the signs of the times, it is helpful to listen to **young people and the elderly**. [108]

Chapter Five

Everyone is Called to Share the Gospel

Pope Francis affirms that the Church is a people on their way to God. Consequently, it is much more than an institution. Nor is the Church an exclusive group; everyone is to be welcomed, loved and forgiven. Nor is the Church bound to one cultural expression. The presence of The Holy Spirit expresses itself in many and different ways, while still guarding unity in love. Experts in all professions help the Church to pass on the good news, and popular piety shows us people's deep desire for God. We must never forget that as a Church we fail unless we speak of Jesus as Lord.

There can be no true evangelisation without the explicit joyful, patient, progressive proclamation of Jesus as Lord. [110]

The Church as the agent of evangelisation, is more than an organic and hierarchical institution. [111]

The Church is first and foremost **a people advancing on its pilgrim way towards God.** [111]

A people for everyone
It is important to know that the first word, **the true initiative and activity comes from God.** [112]

The salvation which God has wrought, and the Church proclaims joyfully, is for everyone … Jesus did **not tell his apostles to form an exclusive and elite group.** [113]

The Church is **God's leaven** in the midst of humanity. [114]

The Church must be a place of mercy freely given where **everyone can feel welcomed,** loved, forgiven, encouraged to live the life of the Gospel. [114]

A people of many faces
The concept of culture is valuable for grasping the various expressions of the Christian life present in God's People. [115]

When properly understood, **cultural diversity** is not a threat to Church unity. [117]

It is not essential **to impose a specific cultural form,** no matter how beautiful or ancient it is, together with the Gospel. [117]

We cannot demand that people of every continent, in expressing their Christian faith, imitate modes of expression which European nations developed at a particular moment in their history. [118]

We are all missionary disciples
In all the baptised ... the sanctifying power of the Spirit, is at work, impelling us to evangelisation. [119]

Anyone who has truly **experienced God's saving love,** does not need much time or lengthy training to go out and proclaim that Love. [120]

Each of us should find a way **to communicate Jesus,** wherever we are ... our falling short of perfection should be no excuse. [121]

The evangelising power of popular piety
Popular piety is an ongoing and developing process, of which the Holy Spirit is the principal agent. [122]

Popular piety manifests a thirst for God which only the poor and the simple can know. [123]

Popular piety discovers and expresses the content [of faith] more by way of **symbols** than by discursive reasoning. [124]

Being a disciple means being constantly **ready to bring the love of Jesus to others** ... on the street, in the city square, during work, on a journey. [127]

The first step is personal dialogue, when the other person speaks and shares his or her joys, hopes and concerns for loved ones. Only afterwards is it possible to bring up God's word. [128]

If the circumstances are right, a fraternal and missionary encounter could end with **a brief prayer.** [128]

This communication [of the Gospel] takes place in so **many different ways** that it would be impossible to describe them all. [129]

Charisms at the Service of an Evangelising Communion
The Holy Spirit also enriches the entire evangelising Church with **different charisms** ...

They are gifts of the Spirit integrated into the body of the Church. [130]

The Holy Spirit alone can raise up **diversity, plurality and multiplicity** while at the same time bringing about unity. [131]

Culture, thought and education
Proclaiming the Gospel message to different cultures also involves proclaiming it to **professional, scientific and academic circles**. [132]

I call on **theologians** to carry out this service – bring the Gospel message to different cultural contexts and groups – as part of the Church's saving mission. [133]

Universities are outstanding environments for articulating and developing this evangelising commitment in an interdisciplinary and integrated way. [134]

Catholic schools … are a most valuable resource for the evangelisation of culture. [134]

Chapter Six

Preaching the Gospel

ere the Pope encourages priests to express
their love for their people in well-prepared,
well-delivered homilies. He expects them
to show clearly how much they enjoy
communicating God's word, as Jesus did. He
reminds priests that the purpose of their preaching
is to join the hearts of their listeners joyfully with
the heart of God. He asks every priest to prepare his
homilies with great care through study, prayer and
creative thinking. Because the words of scripture
have power within them, the Pope asks priests to
help in releasing that power to their listeners.

The homily is the touchstone for judging **a pastor's
closeness and ability to communicate to his people.**
[135]

It is **God who seeks to reach out** to others through
the preacher, and … he displays his power through
human words. [136]

The liturgical context

The liturgical proclamation of the word of God …
is not so much a time for meditation and
catechesis as **a dialogue between God and his
people.** [137]

The preacher must **know the heart of his
community,** in order to realise where its desire for
God is alive and ardent. [137]

[The homily] should be brief and avoid taking on
the semblance of **a speech or a lecture.** [138]

Within the context of the liturgy [the homily] is
part of the offering made to the Father and a
mediation of the grace which Christ pours out
during the celebration. [138]

A mother's conversation

The same **Spirit [of mother-child love]** who
inspired the Gospels and who acts in the Church
also inspires the preacher … at each Eucharist.
[139]

The Lord truly **enjoys talking with his people;** the
preacher should strive to communicate that same
enjoyment to his listeners. [141]

Words which set hearts on fire
Dialogue is much more than the communication
of a truth. It arises from **the enjoyment of speaking**
and it enriches those who express their love for one
another through the medium of words. [142]

The challenge of an inculturated preaching
consists in proclaiming a synthesis, not ideas or
detached values. Where your synthesis is, there lies
your heart. [143]

The preacher has the wonderful but difficult task
of **joining loving hearts,** the heart of the Lord and
his people. [143]

To speak from the heart means that our hearts
must **not just be on fire, but also enlightened** by
the fullness of revelation and by the path travelled
by God's word in the heart of the Church. [144]

Preparation for preaching is so important a task
that **a prolonged time of study, reflection and
pastoral creativity** should be devoted to it. [145]

A preacher who does not prepare is not 'spiritual';
he is dishonest and irresponsible with the gifts he
has received. [145]

Reverence for truth

The first step, after calling upon the Holy Spirit in prayer, is to **give our entire attention to the biblical text,** which needs to be the basis of our preaching. [146]

To interpret a biblical text, we need to be patient … and to give it our time, interest and undivided attention. [146]

Preparation for preaching **requires love.** [146]

The biblical text which we study is **two or three thousand years old**; its language is very different from that which we speak today. [147]

Our most important goal is to discover **its principal message,** the message which gives structure and unity to the text. [147]

We need to relate [the central message] of the text to the teaching of **the entire bible** as handed on by the Church. [148]

One of the defects of a tedious and ineffectual preaching is precisely its inability to transmit **the intrinsic power of the text** which has been proclaimed. [148]

Personalising the word
The preacher ought first of all to develop a great personal familiarity with the word of God. [149]

[The preacher] needs to approach the word with **a docile and prayerful heart** so that it may deeply penetrate his thoughts and feelings and bring about a new outlook in him. [149]

The greater or lesser degree of the **holiness of the minister** has a real effect on the proclamation of the word. [149]

If we have a lively desire to be the **first to hear the word which we preach,** this will surely be communicated to God's faithful people. [149]

Whoever wants to preach must be the first to **let the word of God move him** deeply and become incarnate in his daily life. [150]

Today too, people prefer to listen to witnesses: they thirst for authenticity and call for evangelisers to speak of **a God whom they themselves know.** [150]

We are not asked to be flawless, but to keep growing and wanting to grow as we advance along the path of the Gospel. [151]

What is essential is that **the preacher be certain that God loves him,** that Jesus Christ has saved him and that his love has always the last word. [151]

The Lord wants to make use of us as living, free and creative beings who let **his word enter [our] own hearts** before then passing it on to others. [151]

Christ's message must truly **penetrate and possess the preacher,** not just intellectually but in his entire being. [151]

Spiritual reading
[Lectio divina] consists of reading God's word in a moment of prayer and allowing it to enlighten and renew us. [152]

[A] common temptation is to think about **what the text means [to] other people**. [153]

[God] always invites us to take a step forward, but does not demand a full response if we are not yet ready. [153]

An ear to the people
A preacher has to contemplate the word, but he
also has **to contemplate his people.** [154]

He needs to be able to link the message of a
biblical text to a human situation. [154]

The spiritual sensitivity for reading **God's message
in events** … is much more than simply finding
something interesting to say. [154]

What we are looking for is **what the Lord has to
say** in this or that particular circumstance. [154]

Preparation for preaching [is] an exercise in
evangelical discernment. [154]

Let us also keep in mind that we should never
respond to **questions that nobody asks.** [155]

Some people think they can be good preachers
because they know what ought to be said, but they
pay no attention to *how* **it should be said.** [156]

Homiletic resources
Active love of our neighbour [is shown] by refusing
to offer others **a product of poor quality.** [156]

One of the most important things is to learn how to **use images in preaching**. [157]

A good homily should have an **idea, a sentiment and an image**. [157]

If we wish to adapt to people's language and to reach them with God's word, we need to **share in their lives** and pay loving attention to them. [158]

Another feature of **a good homily is that it is positive**. It is not so much concerned with pointing out what shouldn't be done, but with suggesting what we can do better. [159]

Positive preaching always offers hope, points to the future, does not leave us trapped in negativity. [159]

Chapter Seven

Catechesis and Accompaniment

Here the Pope points out that there is growth in our receiving God's word; it is a gradual process. This growth is not merely a matter of understanding it more, but rather one of receiving it ever more deeply into our hearts. The word of God is beautiful, and every expression of beauty in the world leads us to God. The more we appreciate the beauty of the liturgy, the more it catechises us. The Pope also speaks of the very old tradition of having someone to accompany us on our journey in holiness. Deep respectful listening is necessary as we meet together around God's word in scripture.

The first proclamation [of the Gospel] calls for ongoing **formation and maturation**. [160]

Evangelisation aims at **a process of growth** which entails taking seriously each person and God's plan for his or her life. [160]

It would **not** be right to see this call to growth exclusively or primarily in terms of **doctrinal formation.** [161]

The New Testament authors want to present **the heart of the Christian moral message** – the essential requirement of love for one's neighbour. [161]

The process of response and growth is always preceded by **God's gift** [of Baptism]. [162]

Kerygmatic and mystagogical catechesis
On the lips of the catechist **the first proclamation** must ring out over and over: 'Jesus Christ loves you; he gave his life to save you: and now he is living at your side every day to enlighten, strengthen and free you.' [164]

We must announce [**the first proclamation**] one way or another throughout the process of catechesis, **at every level and moment.** [164]

The priest ... ought to grow in awareness that he himself is continually in need of **being evangelised.** [164]

The centrality of the kerygma … has to express
God's saving **love which precedes any moral and
religious obligation** on our part; I should not
impose the truth but appeal to freedom. [165]

[The evangeliser must have] an attitude that
fosters openness to the message: approachability,
readiness for dialogue, patience, a warmth and
welcome that is non-judgemental. [165]

Mystagogic initiation that has developed in recent
decades, has to do with a progressive experience of
formation involving the entire community and a
renewed appreciation of the liturgical signs of
Christian initiation. [166]

Every form of catechesis would do well to attend
to **'the way of beauty'** … Showing that to believe in
and to follow [Christ] is not only something right
and true, but also something beautiful. [167]

Every expression of true beauty can be
acknowledged as a path leading to an encounter
with the Lord Jesus. [167]

It is helpful to stress again and again the
attractiveness and the ideal of **a life of wisdom,
self-fulfilment and enrichment**. [168]

Rather than experts in dire predictions, dour judges bent on rooting out every threat and deviation, we should appear as joyful messengers of challenging proposals, **guardians of the goodness and beauty** which shine forth in a life of fidelity to the Gospel. [168]

Personal accompaniment processes of growth
The Church will have to initiate everyone – priests, religious and laity – into **this art of accompaniment** which teaches us to remove our sandals before the sacred ground of the other. [169]

The pace of this accompaniment must be steady and reassuring, reflecting our closeness and **our compassionate gaze** which also heals, liberates and encourages growth in the Christian life. [169]

Spiritual accompaniment must lead others ever closer to God, in whom we attain **true freedom**. [170]

Some people think they are free if they can **avoid God**; they fail to see that they remain existentially orphaned, helpless, homeless. They cease being pilgrims and become drifters. [170]

To accompany them would be counterproductive if it became **a sort of therapy** supporting their self-absorption and ceased to be a pilgrimage with Christ to the Father. [170]

Listening, in communication, is an openness of heart which makes possible that closeness without which genuine spiritual encounter cannot occur. [171]

Listening helps us to find **the right gesture and word** which shows that we are more than simply bystanders. [171]

Anyone can have grace and charity, and yet **falter in the exercise of the virtues** because of persistent contrary inclinations. [171]

[We need] a pedagogy which will introduce people step by step to the **full appropriation of the mystery.** [171]

Each person's situation before God and their life in grace are mysteries which no one can fully know from without. [172]

The Gospel tells us **to correct others** and to help them to grow on the basis of a recognition of the objective evil of their actions, but without making judgements about their responsibility and culpability. [172]

Our personal experience of being accompanied and assisted, and of openness to those who accompany us, will teach us to be **patient and compassionate with others,** and to find the right way to gain their trust, their openness and readiness to grow. [172]

[Spiritual accompaniment] is clearly distinct from every kind of **intrusive accompaniment** or isolated self-realisation. Missionary disciples accompany missionary disciples. [173]

Centred on the word of God
All evangelisation is based on [the Word of God], listened to, meditated upon, lived, celebrated and witnessed to. **The sacred Scriptures** are the very source of evangelisation. [174]

The preaching of the word, living and effective, prepares for the reception of the sacrament, and in the sacrament that word attains its maximum efficacy. [174]

Chapter Eight

The Gospel in Society

Pope Francis states clearly that the Church does not exist for itself. Its purpose is to build up God's kingdom in the world by building it in peoples' hearts and among them. In this way, he says that Jesus lives again in each of us when we receive and accept God's word. St Paul described the kingdom as a place of 'saving justice, peace and joy brought by the Holy Spirit'. The Pope stresses that God's message is not just about our individual relationships with one another. It equally calls for justice and love in every aspect of society.

To evangelise is to make the kingdom of God present in our world. [176]

The content of the first proclamation has an immediate moral implication centred on charity. [177]

Confession of faith and commitment to society
To believe in a Father who loves all men and
women with an infinite love means realising that
he thereby confers upon them **an infinite dignity**.
[178]

To believe that the Son of God assumed our
human flesh means that each human person has
been taken up **into the very heart of God**. [178]

To believe that the Holy Spirit is at work in
everyone means realising that he seeks **to penetrate
every human situation**. [178]

Evangelisation is meant to cooperate with [the]
liberating work of the Spirit. [178]

Our brothers and sisters are **the prolongation of
the incarnation** for each of us. [179]

The Kingdom and its challenge
Reading the Scriptures ... makes it clear that the
Gospel is **not merely about our personal
relationship with God**. [180]

Our personal relationship to God ... should not be
seen simply as **an accumulation of small personal
gestures** to individuals in need. [180]

To the extent that [God] reigns within us, the life of society will be a setting for **universal fraternity, justice, peace and dignity**. [180]

Both Christian preaching and life, then, are meant to have an **impact on society**. [180]

The Church's teaching on social questions
God wants his children **to be happy in this world** too … for he has created all things for our enjoyment, the enjoyment of *everyone*. [182]

An authentic faith … always involves a deep desire to change the world, to transmit values, **to leave this earth somehow better than we found it**. [183]

The Church cannot and must not remain on the sidelines **in the fight for justice**. [183]

It is up to **Christian communities to analyse** with objectivity the situation which is proper to their own country. [184]

Chapter Nine

Primacy of the Poor in Society

Central to Pope Francis' call for a transformed Church is his emphasis on the Church's need to care spiritually and materially for the poor. By 'poor', he means those who are deprived of their basic rights in any way through having been pushed to the edge of society. When this takes place, God's plan is not being fulfilled. This is often done indirectly by rich or powerful persons who create structures which ensure that others cannot get justice in society. The Church and individual Christians must identify with these deprived groups, these poor, as Jesus did. They must also protect the fragile natural world in which we live.

Our faith in Christ, who became poor, and was always close to the poor and the outcast, is the basis of our concern for the integral development of **society's most neglected members.** [186]

In union with God, we hear a plea
Each individual Christian and every community is
called to be an instrument of God for the
liberation and promotion of the poor. [187]

'**How does God's love abide** in anyone who has the
world's goods, and sees a brother or sister in need
and yet refuses help?' *John 3:17* [187]

[Hearing the Gospel] means working **to eliminate
the structural causes of poverty** and to promote
the integral development of the poor, as well as
small daily acts of solidarity in meeting the real
needs which we encounter. [188]

[The Gospel] presumes the creation of a new
mindset that thinks in terms of community and
the **priority of the life of all over appropriation of
goods by the few.** [188]

Changing structures without generating **new
convictions and attitudes** will only ensure that
those same structures will become … corrupt,
oppressive and ineffectual. [189]

The more fortunate should **renounce some of their
rights** so as to place their goods more generously at
the service of others. [190]

There is **enough food for everyone** and that
hunger is the result of a poor distribution of goods
and income. The problem is made worse by the
generalised practice of wastefulness. [191]

We are not simply talking about ensuring
nourishment ... but also ... **education, access to
healthcare and above all employment.** [192]

Fidelity to the Gospel, lest we run in vain
We incarnate the duty of hearing the cry of the
poor when we are **deeply moved by the suffering of
others.** [193]

The apostle James teaches us that **our mercy to
others** will vindicate us on the day of God's
judgement. [193]

Whenever we have an opportunity to perform a
work of **mercy,** we should **rejoice.** [193]

The message [of mercy] is so clear and direct, so
simple and eloquent, that no ecclesial
interpretation has **the right to relativise it** ... or to
obscure or weaken [its] force. [194]

We should not be concerned simply about falling into doctrinal error, but **about remaining faithful** to this light-filled path of life and wisdom. [194]

We may not always be able to reflect adequately the beauty of the Gospel, but there is **one sign which we should never lack**: the option for those who are least, those whom society discards. [195]

Sometimes **we prove hard of heart and mind**; we are forgetful, distracted and carried away by the limitless possibilities for consumption and distraction offered by contemporary society. [196]

The special place of the poor in God's people
God's heart has a special place for the poor, so much so that **he himself became poor.** [197]

I want a church that is **poor and for the poor**. [198]

Our commitment does not consist exclusively in activities and programmes of promotion and assistance … but above all an attentiveness which considers **the other in a certain sense as one with ourselves.** [199]

Only on the basis of ... **real and sincere closeness** can we properly accompany the poor on their path of liberation. [199]

The worst discrimination which the poor suffer is the **lack of spiritual care**. [200]

None of us can think we are exempt from concern for the poor and for social justice. [201]

The economy and the distribution of income
The need to resolve **the structural causes of poverty** cannot be delayed ... because society needs to be cured of a sickness which is weakening it. [202]

The dignity of each human person and the pursuit of the common good are concerns which ought to shape **all economic policies**. [203]

We can no longer trust in the **unseen forces** and the invisible hand of the market. [204]

I ask God to give us more **politicians** ... who are genuinely disturbed by the state of society ... capable of sincere and effective dialogue aimed at healing ... the evils in our world! [205]

It is becoming increasingly **difficult to find local solutions** for [the] enormous global problems which overwhelm local politics with difficulties to resolve. [206]

Without creative concern in ... helping the poor [a church community], however much it may talk about social issues and criticise governments ... will easily drift into spiritual worldliness **camouflaged by religious practices,** unproductive meetings and empty talk. [207]

If anyone feels offended by my words, I would respond that **I speak them with affection** and with the best of intentions. My words are not those of a foe or an opponent. [208]

Concern for the vulnerable
The current model, with its **emphasis on success and self-reliance,** does not appear to favour an investment in efforts to help the slow, the weak or the less talented. [209]

It is essential to draw near to **new forms of poverty** and vulnerability, in which we are called to recognise the suffering Christ. [210]

I am pastor of **a Church without frontiers,** a Church which considers herself mother to all. [210]

The infamous network of crime – human trafficking – is now well established in our cities, and many people have **blood on their hands** as a result of their comfortable and silent complicity. [211]

Doubly poor are those **women who endure situations of exclusion, mistreatment and violence,** since they are frequently less able to defend their rights. [212]

Among the vulnerable for whom the Church wishes to care with particular love and concern are **unborn children.** [213]

We have done little to adequately accompany **women in very difficult situations,** where abortion appears as a quick solution to their profound anguish. [214]

There are other weak and defenceless beings who are frequently at the mercy of economic interests or **indiscriminate exploitation.** I am speaking of creation as a whole. [215]

We human beings are not only the beneficiaries but also the stewards of other creatures … **The desertification of the soil … and the extinction of a species** are a painful disfigurement. [215]

All of us, as Christians, are called to watch over and **protect the fragile world** in which we live, and all its peoples. [216]

Chapter Ten

The Common Good and Peace in Society

Here the Pope reminds us that peace is vital for the welfare of any society. If any system silences groups within it in the name of peace, there is injustice. If the privileges of rich groups result in a lack of opportunity for integral development in the poor, Christians must speak out. He also calls for participation in public life by all believers. This process of people-building takes time, and any conflict which emerges must be faced by action and not merely by words. Sometimes this action must be taken on the local level, and sometimes on the global.

True peace [does not] act as a pretext for justifying a social structure which silences or appeases the poor, so that the more affluent can placidly support their lifestyle. [218]

The dignity of the human person ... ranks higher than the comfort of those who refuse to renounce their privileges. When ... values are threatened, a prophetic voice must be raised. [218]

In the end, a **peace** which is not the result of integral development will be doomed. [219]

Participation in public life is a moral obligation. [220]

Time is greater than space
Time has to do with fullness as an expression of the horizon which constantly opens before us, while each individual moment has to do with limitation as an expression of enclosure. [222]

[We need to generate] processes of **people-building**, as opposed to obtaining immediate results which yield easy, quick short-term political gains, but do not enhance human fullness. [224]

Evangelisation ... calls for attention to **the bigger picture**, openness to suitable processes and concern for the long run. [225]

Unity prevails over conflict
Conflict cannot be ignored or concealed. It has to be faced. But if we remain in conflict, we lose our perspective, our horizons shrink and reality itself begins to fall apart. [226]

[We need a] willingness to **face conflict head on,** to resolve it and to make it a link in the chain of a new process. 'Blessed are the peacemakers!' *Matthew 5:9* [227]

Communion amid disagreement ... can only be achieved by those great persons who are willing to **go beyond the surface** of the conflict and to see others in their deepest dignity. [228]

The locus [to] **reconciliation of differences is within ourselves,** in our own lives, ever threatened as they are by fragmentation and breakdown. [229]

Realities are more important than ideas
It is dangerous to dwell in **the realm of words alone, of images and rhetoric** ... Realities are greater than ideas. This calls for rejecting the various means [the Pope offers eight] of masking reality. [231]

[People do not follow some] politicians and religious leaders ... because they are stuck in the **realm of pure ideas** and end up reducing politics or faith to rhetoric. [232]

[The Gospel] impels us to put **the word into practice,** to perform works of justice and charity which make [the] word fruitful. [233]

The whole is greater than the part
We need to pay attention to **the global** so as to avoid narrowness and banality. Yet we also need to look to **the local,** which keeps our feet on the ground. [234]

People get caught up in **an abstract, globalised universe,** falling into step behind everyone else, admiring the glitter of other people's world. [234]

At the other extreme, they turn into **a museum of local folklore,** a world apart … to doing the same things over and over … incapable of … appreciating the beauty which God bestows beyond their borders. [234]

The global need not stifle, nor **the particular** prove barren. [235]

It is **the sum total of persons within** a society which pursues the common good, which truly has a place for everyone. [236]

The Church passes down to us and sends us forth to proclaim [**the polyhedron principle** on many levels] in prayer, fraternity, justice, struggle and celebration. [237]

Chapter Eleven

The Role of Dialogue in Creating Peace

The Pope repeatedly stresses Jesus' central message, when he says, 'Blessed are the peacemakers ...' In being a peacemaker – not just a peacekeeper – the Church and its members are called to dialogue with others. The Church has nothing to fear from speaking with reasonable people. Having so much in common with Christians of other traditions gives us a strong motive for respectful dialogue. We speak in a brotherly way with the Jewish people, with whom we share so much of the Scriptures and their faith in Abraham; and the Islamic people and we can come closer to each other. The Church can learn from and work with non-believers who follow their consciences.

Evangelisation involves ... dialogue with states, dialogue with society ... cultures, the sciences and other believers ... keeping ever in mind the life and sufferings of human beings. [238]

The new evangelisation calls on **every baptised person to be a peacemaker** and a credible witness to a reconciled life. [239]

Based on the principles of subsidiarity and solidarity, it is **the responsibility of the State** to safeguard and promote the common good of society. [240]

Dialogue between faith, reason and science
Faith is not fearful of reason; on the contrary, it seeks and trusts reason, since the light of reason and the light of faith both come from God. [242]

Whenever **the sciences** ... arrive at a conclusion which reason cannot refute, faith does not contradict it. [243]

Ecumenical dialogue
The credibility of the Christian message would be much greater if Christians could overcome their divisions. [244]

[Christians] are pilgrims journeying alongside one another. This means that we must have **sincere trust in our fellow pilgrims**. [244]

[If we Christians] **concentrate on the convictions we share,** and if we keep in mind the principle of the hierarchy of truths, we will be able to progress decidedly towards common expressions of proclamation, service and witness. [246]

We Catholics have the opportunity to learn more about the meaning of episcopal collegiality and their **experience of synodality** ... with our Orthodox brothers and sisters. [246]

Relations with Judaism
The Church, which **shares with Jews an important part of the sacred Scriptures,** looks upon the people of the covenant and their faith as on the sacred roots of her own Christian identity. [247]

The friendship which has grown between us [and the Jewish people] makes us bitterly and **sincerely regret the terrible persecutions** which they have endured ... especially those that have involved Christians. [248]

The Church ... is enriched when she receives the values of Judaism. [249]

Interreligious dialogue

An attitude of openness in truth and in love must characterise the dialogue with the followers of **non-Christian religions**, in spite of forms … of fundamentalism on both sides. [250]

In this dialogue [with non-Christian religions], ever friendly and sincere, attention must always be paid to the essential bond between **dialogue and proclamation**. [251]

Together with us [**the followers of Islam**] adore the one, merciful God, who will judge humanity on the last day. [252]

Christians should embrace with affection and respect **Muslim immigrants** to our countries in the same way that we hope and ask to be received and respected in countries of Islamic tradition. [253]

Non-Christians, by God's gracious initiative, when they are faithful to their own consciences, can live justified by the grace of God, and thus be associated to the paschal mystery of Jesus Christ. [254]

Social dialogues in a context of religious freedom
[The fundamental human right to religious freedom] includes **the freedom to choose** the religion which one judges to be true and to manifest one's beliefs in public. [255]

Intellectuals and serious journalists frequently descend to **crude and superficial generalisations** in speaking of the shortcomings of religion. [256]

We … feel close to **those who do not consider themselves part of any religious tradition,** yet sincerely seek the truth, goodness and beauty which we believe have their highest expression and source in God. [257]

Believers and non-believers are able to engage in dialogue about fundamental issues of ethics, art and science, and about the search for transcendence. [257]

[There is an] **inescapable social dimension** [to] the Gospel message [and I encourage] all Christians to demonstrate it by their words, attitudes and deeds. [258]

Chapter Twelve

A New Spirit-filled Mission

Reminding us of the obvious, the Pope points out that dissertations or a vague spirituality will not motivate believers to work at bringing others to God. Authentic prayer, especially around God's word and the Eucharist, gives us the reasons, the energy and the love to do this work. We meet God more fully when we are actively concerned and working for their integral welfare. Too much concern for our ease or for luxury, rather than for the suffering and total welfare of others, will destroy us. Underlying all our efforts is the conviction that we are supported by the power of the risen Jesus.

Spirit-filled evangelisers means evangelisers fearlessly **open to the working of the Holy Spirit** … [who] also grant the courage to proclaim the newness of the Gospel with boldness. [259]

Without prayer, all our activity risks being fruitless, and our message empty. Spirit-filled evangelisers are evangelisers who **pray and work**. [259]+[262]

Mystical notions without a solid social and missionary outreach are of no help to evangelisation. [262]

Dissertations or social or pastoral practices which lack a spirituality which can change hearts are of no help to evangelisation. [262]

The Church urgently needs the deep breath of prayer ... **prayerful reading of God's word and the perpetual adoration of the Eucharist** ... at every level of ecclesial life. [262]

There is always the risk that **some moments of prayer can become an excuse** for not offering one's life in mission ... and can lead Christians to take refuge in some false form of spirituality. [262]

Every period of history is marked by the presence of **human weakness,** self-absorption, complacency and selfishness ... and concupiscence which preys upon us all. [263]

Personal encounter with the saving love of Jesus
The primary reason for evangelising is the love of Jesus which we have received. What kind of love would not feel the need to speak of the beloved? [264]

The best incentive for sharing the Gospel comes from contemplating it with love ... We need to recover a contemplative spirit which can help us to realise ever anew that we have been entrusted with a treasure. [264]

Sometimes we lose our enthusiasm for mission because we forget that the Gospel responds to our deepest needs, since we were created for ... friendship with Jesus and love of our brothers and sisters. [265]

There already exists in individuals and peoples **an expectation,** even if an unconscious one, of knowing the truth about God, about man, and about how we are to be set free from sin and death. [265]

Our infinite sadness can only be cured by **an infinite love** ... This conviction has to be sustained by our own constantly renewed experience of savouring Christ's friendship. [255]+[256]

A true missionary, who never ceases to be a disciple, knows that **Jesus walks with him,** speaks to him, breathes with him, works with him. [266]

A person who is not convinced, enthusiastic, certain and in love, will convince nobody. [266]

If we wish to commit ourselves fully and
perseveringly, we need to leave behind every other
motivation. [267]

The spiritual savour of being a people
To be evangelisers of souls, we need to develop a
spiritual taste for being **close to people's lives** and
to discover that this is itself a source of greater joy.
[268]

Mission is **at once a passion for Jesus** and **a passion
for people.** [268]

[Jesus] sends us to his people. He wants to make
use of us to draw closer to his beloved people …
without this **sense of belonging** we cannot
understand our deepest identity. [268]

Moved by the example of Jesus, we want to **enter
fully into the fabric of society,** sharing the lives of all
… not from a sense of obligation but [from] a
personal decision which brings joy to our lives. [269]

Sometimes we are tempted to be that kind of
Christian who keeps the Lord's wounds at arm's
length. Yet Jesus wants us to **touch … the suffering
flesh of others.** [270]

[Jesus] hopes that we will stop looking for those personal and communal niches which shelter us from the maelstrom of human misfortune and instead **enter into the reality of other people's lives** and know the power of tenderness. [270]

Clearly, Jesus does not want us to be grandees who look down upon others, but **men and women of the people.** [271]

One who does not love others 'walks in the darkness' (*1 John 2:11*), 'remains in death' (*1 John 3:14*) and 'does not know God' (*1 John 4:8*). [272]

Whenever we encounter another person in love, we learn something new about God … we grow in the light of faith. [272]

Only the person who feels happiness in **seeking the good of others,** in desiring their happiness, can be a missionary. [272]

We have to regard ourselves as sealed, even **branded, by this mission** of bringing light, blessing, enlivening, raising up, healing and freeing. [273]

If we are to share our lives with others … we have to realise that **every person is worthy of our giving** … He or she reflects God's glory. [274]

We achieve fulfilment when we break down walls and **our heart is filled with faces and names!** [274]

The mysterious working of the risen Christ and his Spirit
'Why should I deny myself **my comforts and pleasures** if I won't see any significant results?' ... [This] is a self-destructive attitude. [275]

Christ's resurrection is not an event of the past; it contains a vital power which has permeated this world. [276]

Often it seems that God does not exist: all around us we see persistent injustice, evil, indifference and cruelty ... However dark things are, **goodness always re-emerges** and spreads. [276]

Our hearts can tire of the struggle because in the end we are caught up in ourselves, in a careerism that thirsts for recognition, applause, rewards and status. [277]

[Faith] means believing that **[God] marches triumphantly in history** with those who 'are called and chosen and faithful'. (*Revelation 17:14*) [278]

The kingdom is here, it returns, it struggles to flourish anew. Christ's resurrection everywhere calls forth seeds of [a] new world; even if they are cut back, they grow again. [278]

Because we do not always see these seeds [of the kingdom] growing, we need an interior certainty, a conviction that God is able to act in every situation, even amid **apparent setbacks**. [279]

Fruitfulness is often invisible, elusive and unquantifiable. We can know quite well that our lives will be fruitful, without claiming to know how, or where, or when ... none of our acts of love will be lost. [279]

Keeping our missionary fervour alive calls for firm **trust in the Holy Spirit** ... so we need to invoke the Spirit constantly. [280]

There is no greater freedom than that of allowing oneself to be guided by the Holy Spirit, renouncing the attempt to plan and control everything to the last detail. [280]

The missionary power of intercessory prayer
One form of prayer moves us particularly to take
up the task of evangelisation and to seek the good
of others: it is **the prayer of intercession**. [281]

[Our] prayer of gratitude to God for others ... is a
spiritual gaze born of deep faith which
acknowledges what God is doing in the lives of
others. [281]

[God] is always there first, [but] what our
intercession achieves is that his power, his love and
his faithfulness are shown ever more clearly in the
midst of his people. [283]

Chapter Thirteen

Mary,
Mother of Evangelisation

Realistically, Pope Francis encourages us with the reminder that we will not always see the results we hope for. We will always have moments of darkness and of doubt. Mary endured similar discouraging moments in her life. She was given to us by Jesus as our mother when he spoke to John from the cross. We can be inspired by her life and rely on the help of her motherly love in bringing the joy of the Gospel ever more fully into our own hearts and into the hearts of others.

[Mary] joined the disciples in praying for the coming of the Holy Spirit and thus made possible the missionary outburst which took place at Pentecost. [284]

Jesus' gift to his people
Jesus left us his mother to be our mother … The
Lord did not want to leave the Church without
this icon of womanhood. [285]

She is the friend who is ever concerned **that wine
not be lacking** in our lives. [286]

As mother of [us] all, she is a sign of **hope for
peoples suffering** the birth pangs of justice. [286]

Star of the new evangelisation
We ask the Mother of the living Gospel to
intercede that this **invitation to a new phase of
evangelisation** will be accepted by the entire
ecclesial community. [287]

Along [the] journey of evangelisation we will have
our **moments of aridity, darkness and even fatigue.**
Mary herself experienced these things during the
years of Jesus' childhood. [287]

Mary, for many years, lived in intimacy with the
mystery of her Son, and went **forward in her
pilgrimage** of faith. [287]

Whenever we look to Mary, we come to believe once again in the **revolutionary nature of love and tenderness**. [288]

The interplay of **justice and tenderness, of contemplation and concern for others,** is what makes the ecclesial community look to Mary as a model of evangelisation. [288]

Selected Index